The Bexhill West Branch 1

Peter A. Ha

GW00671683

H class 0-4-4T No. 31269 with the branch train at Bexhill West Station. June 30th 1956.

R.M. Casserley

Published by Peter A. Harding,
"Mossgiel", Bagshot Road, Knaphill,
Woking, Surrey GU21 2SG.

ISBN 0 9523458 6 2

© Peter A. Harding 2002.
Printed by Binfield Print & Design Ltd.,
Binfield Road, Byfleet Village, Surrey KT14 7PN

Contents

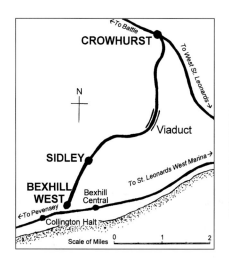

H class 0-4-4T No. 31274 with the branch train heading north towards Crowhurst after crossing over the viaduct. May 11th 1957. Denis Cullum

Pull-and-push unit No.661 with H class 0-4-4T No. 31162 at Sidley Station, March 2nd 1955. Denis Cullum

Introduction

The 4½ mile railway from Crowhurst to Bexhill via Sidley was opened with great enthusiasm on May 31st 1902 at a private ceremony. The following day, the line was opened to the public. Work had started on the construction in January 1898 and the main reason that such a short line should take so long to build was a 17 arch viaduct which was needed to cross the valley and over the marshes between Crowhurst and Sidley.

By connecting with the main London-Hastings line at Crowhurst, the new line offered a more direct route from Bexhill to London than the original coastal line that the London Brighton & South Coast Railway had opened from Lewes through Bexhill to Bulverhythe near St. Leonards on June 27th 1846. With the people of Bexhill hoping that their town would develop into one of the main health resorts on the south coast, this more direct route was seen as a great advantage.

Unfortunately, after the initial enthusiasm at the opening, the new line failed to attract that many passengers away from the original line and when the newly formed Southern Railway inherited both lines at the 1923 grouping, they decided to call the original station Bexhill Central and appeared to give it more importance. The newer station eventually received the title of Bexhill West and perhaps that was the very reason that the line did not catch on, as it was situated on the western side of the town while Bexhill Central was, as the title suggests, more central.

The Crowhurst to Bexhill West line closed on June 14th 1964 and although it only lasted 62 years, it was still of great interest and I hope that readers will be able to capture some of the character of this railway which started life as an important link with London and finished as a simple country branch line.

H class 0-4-4T No. 31162 waits in the down branch bay at Crowhurst Station ready to propel the branch train to Bexhill West, April 12th 1958.   D.W. Winkworth

History of the Line

In 1844 the Brighton, Lewes & Hastings Railway obtained authority to build a line from Brighton to Hastings via Bexhill, and under the same Act to sell the undertaking to the London & Brighton Railway. At that time, the Sussex seaside resort of Bexhill was still only a small fishing community on the coast while the village of Bexhill stood on a hill about a mile inland. The first section of this line from Brighton to Lewes opened on June 8th 1846 while the section from Lewes through Bexhill to Bulverhythe near St. Leonards opened on June 27th 1846. The London & Brighton Railway amalgamated with the London & Croydon Railway on July 27th 1846 to become the London Brighton & South Coast Railway (LB&SCR). A short extension from Bulverhythe to West Marina at St. Leonards opened on November 7th 1846.

The LB&SCR opened a new line from their main London to Brighton line south of Wivelsfield at Keymer Junction to Lewes on October 27th 1847 which gave direct access to London from St. Leonards, while a branch to Eastbourne was opened on May 14th 1849 from Polegate, which was about half way between Lewes and St. Leonards.

An extension from St. Leonards to Hastings, Rye and Ashford had also been sanctioned although this was later transferred to the South Eastern Railway (SER) who built and opened the line through to Ashford on February 13th 1851. The SER also built a line from their main London to Dover line at Tonbridge to Hastings via Tunbridge Wells and Battle which opened on February 1st 1852 and gave direct access to London from Hastings. The LB&SCR line from West Marina at St. Leonards joined the SER at a new junction called Bopeep.

At this time, despite having a railway station, Bexhill had still not developed into a seaside resort compared with their neighbours Eastbourne and Hastings. Towards the latter part of the nineteenth century, prompted by the 8th Earl De La Warr who was a major landowner in the area, it was decided to try and develop Bexhill into one of the leading health resorts in the South of England. One slight disadvantage was the lack of a more direct rail route to London. Passengers considered it unfortunate that they either had to take the LB&SCR route via Lewes or change at Hastings and travel on the SER line via Tonbridge.

The ill-fated Ouse Valley line which the LB&SCR had planned in 1863 to run from their main London to Brighton line north of Haywards Heath to Uckfield, with extensions to Hailsham and Bexhill would have no doubt given a quicker route to the capital but, unfortunately, even though construction had started, the LB&SCR ran into financial problems and the line was abandoned. At about the same time, a branch to Bexhill from the main SER line just south of Battle at a point called Forward, had also been proposed but never materialised.

With Earl De La Warr's plans to develop the area really starting to take place in the 1880's, a Bexhill Direct Railway from Battle with Charles Beedon King and Joseph A. Bone as the engineers was proposed in 1884 and again in 1885 with access to Eastbourne but still nothing came of these plans or similar plans in 1889.

In 1896 the nominally independent Crowhurst, Sidley & Bexhill Railway (CS&BR) was promoted by local landowners and businessmen who apart from Earl De La Warr also included Mr. John Edwards, Mr. Cranston Leslie, Mr. Albert Parks, Mr. James Cook. Sir Anchitel Piers Ashburnham and Mr. Pelham Rawston Papillon.

Earl De La Warr

These gentlemen plus other subscribers all put money up to build a line from the SER London and Hastings line south of Battle near the small village of Crowhurst where a new station would be built, and from where the new line would leave the main SER line and run across the valley and marshes to Sidley and terminate at Bexhill which was 4½ miles in length. This new line had the full backing of the SER who were quite prepared to advance the CS&BR a substantial loan to get things moving and agreed to work the line using SER rolling stock. The authorised capital was £135,000 with borrowing power of £45,000 on mortgage and although this seemed a large amount of money for such a short line, it must be pointed out that to cross the marshes, it would take a 17 arch viaduct while deep cuttings south of Crowhurst and at Sidley were also required.

The Royal Assent for the construction of the line was obtained on July 15th 1897 and although the CS&BR company registered office was London Bridge Station, the first board meeting was held on July 22nd 1897 at the Charing Cross Hotel, London. The first appointed board of directors consisted of: Sir George Russell, Bart M.P. (Chairman), Henry Cosmo Orme Bonsor, M.P. (Deputy Chairman), the Hon. Alfred Erskine Gathorne-Hardy, Sir Anchitel Piers Ashburnham and Pelham Rawston Papillon. The influence of the SER was there for all to see as Sir George Russell was also Chairman of the SER, while Henry Cosmo Orme Bonsor was the SER Deputy Chairman and the Hon. Alfred Erskine Gathorne-Hardy was also a SER Director. Sir Anchitel Piers Ashburnham was for some time chairman of the Hastings County Bench under whose jurisdiction Bexhill formerly came. He later added the name Clement to his surname and became Sir Anchitel Piers Ashburnham-Clement. Pelham Rawston Papillon was a member of the Papillon family who lived at Crowhurst Park and from whom the CS&BR bought some land for their new line, including the area where Crowhurst Station was built.

Mr. W.R. Stevens the SER Company Secretary attended the first board meeting although Mr. C. Sheath the SER Deputy Secretary was appointed the CS&BR Secretary.

By the beginning of October 1897 the CS&BR had received a loan of £10,000 from the SER.

The company appointed Arthur John Barry of 21, Delahay Street, Westminster, S.W. and Percy Crosland Tempest chief engineer of the SER as their joint engineers and J.C. Bruce as the resident engineer. The contract to build the line was given to John Price of 15, Great George Street, Westminster, S.W. whose firm later became Price & Reeves while the line was in fact being built. The resident agent to the contractors was Mr. F.H. English while the joint surveyors were Mr. G. Humphreys-Davies and Mr. J. Runault. Messrs. Cheeseman and Cope of 3, Great George Street, Westminster, S.W. were appointed solicitors to the company.

With such a task involved in constructing the line, about 700 navvies were for a long time engaged on the work. Most of them were provided with living accommodation in special wooden dwellings at Crowhurst, while some took lodgings in Sidley and Bexhill. On the whole, the navvies showed exemplary behaviour. At Crowhurst they were provided with a special canteen, the profits going to the East Sussex Hospital, while a Sick Benefit Fund was subscribed to in the case of accident or illness. Needless to say that several men sustained severe injuries.

Some preliminary work was done in the latter part of 1897 in the way of clearing the ground and construction of the new line was started in January 1898. The earthwork was described as "heavy in character through Weald clays and Ashdown sands". Seven engines were used at various times by Price & Reeves for the work, six of them receiving local names. They were Manning Wardle 0-6-0 saddle tanks

"Bexhill", "Sidley", "Battle" and "St. Leonards", Manning Wardle 0-4-0 saddle tank "Crowhurst" and Hunslet Engine Co. 0-6-0 saddle tank "Hastings". The odd name out was Manning Wardle 0-6-0 saddle tank "Gosport" which was used on a previous contract by John Price.

The CS&BR Chairman Sir George Russell died on March 7th 1898 and was replaced as Chairman by Henry Cosmo Orme Bonsor on April 28th 1898. Bonsor also replaced Russell as Chairman of the SER. At the same time, Col. John James Mellor, a director of the SER joined the CS&BR board.

Surprisingly, even while all this was happening, a Bexhill & Rotherfield Railway with George Levick as the engineer was also projected in 1898 and again in 1899, although this proposal was later dropped.

With construction of the CS&BR taking place at the Crowhurst end of the line, steps were taken to complete the compulsory purchase of land at Bexhill as authorised by the Act of Parliament. At this time it was at the height of the Bexhill land boom and the CS&BR had to pay heavily. The owner of Bragg's Wood, where the terminus was planned, wanted more than was originally agreed and the company even looked at terminating at Belle Hill. Another suggestion for the terminus came from Mr. John Barker of Grays Inn, London who was interested in some land at Collingwood (¾ of a mile from Bexhill) and thought that the line might be deviated so as to accommodate Collingwood and avoid Bragg's Wood. After some discussion, the matter went to arbitration which took place at the Surveyors' Institute, London and the company agreed to pay a sum of £20,540 for the Bragg's Wood site plus a few other payments which included £5,800 for Wakeham's Farm at Sidley.

With all this extra expense involved, the company were further authorised to borrow £48,000 under an Act of July 1st 1898, plus £16,000 on mortgage.

Later in the same year, Earl De La Warr who as previously mentioned was one of the original promoters of the line, expressed a wish to join the CS&BR board so that the Bexhill end of the line could be represented. With this in mind, he wrote the following letter to H. Cosmo O. Bonsor:-

The Manor House,
Bexhill, Sussex.
November 3rd 1898

Dear Mr. Bonsor,

I should very much like if it can be arranged, to join the Crowhurst & Bexhill Railway Co and thought I would write to you about it. I was, as you may perhaps know, one of the original promoters of the Bill and paid a contribution towards the expenses connected therewith but owing to the attitude taken by the Brighton Railway Company I was practically compelled to withdraw my active support, but not my contribution. I was promised by the Brighton Railway various improvements in our Bexhill train service, and many other benefits which still remain as promised, in consideration for which I agreed to withhold my active support in the promotion of the Bill.

I have been thinking lately that the Crowhurst & Bexhill Railway has no representative on the Board from Bexhill, which is the most important town on the line, and considering the fact that I have a very large interest in the town upon the development of which I am sparing no expense, also considering that hitherto, I think I may say, its progress, it would not be considered too premature on my part to express a wish to join the Board, especially as I know that I could be the means of bringing to it a large amount of traffic both goods and passenger.

I have had a talk with Mr. Willis (*General Manager of the SER*) on the subject and he suggested that I should write to you. I should be very grateful if you could arrange it as I wish, needless to say, I should take a great interest in the line. With apologies for troubling you.

I am
Yours very truly
De La Warr

H. Cosmo O. Bonsor was quick to reply with the following letter:

Kingswood Warren
Epsom.
November 5th 1898

My dear De La Warr,

You certainly will be the right man in the right place on the Board of the Crowhurst & Bexhill Line and I shall have much pleasure in proposing you at the next meeting of the Board. It is only fair that I should tell you that the duties are not heavy and that as I presume the South Eastern will some day absorb the undertaking, your term of office may not be a long one. I am sure however it will be an agreeable one to all of us.

Yours faithfully
H. Cosmo O. Bonsor

Earl De La Warr replied on November 7th 1898 thanking Bonsor for promising to propose him for the Board of the CS&BR but perhaps rather impatiently he wrote to Bonsor again on November 17th 1898 saying that he was sorry to bother him but wondered when he could expect to hear about joining the Board. Bonsor sent the following reply:

Kingswood Warren
Epsom.
November 19th 1898

My dear De La Warr,

The position is that I have told Mr. Sheath the secretary that at the next Board Meeting I will resign my seat in your favour and I will ask him to let you know when the next Board Meeting will be.

Your faithfully
H. Cosmo O. Bonsor

This reply seemed to satisfy Earl De La Warr who answered with the following:

The Manor House,
Bexhill.
November 24th 1898

Dear Bonsor,

Many thanks for your letter of 19th instant.

It is very good of you to resign your seat in my favour, but I am very sorry that I shall not have the pleasure of sitting with you.

Yours very truly
De La Warr

Bonsor did in fact resign from the CS&BR Board and on March 1st 1899 Earl De La Warr was elected. At the same time the Hon. Alfred Erskine Gathorne-Hardy became the new Chairman. Gathorne-Hardy was the 3rd son of the Earl of Cranbrook and second younger brother of Lord Medway and, was at the same time Chairman of the Cranbrook & Paddock Wood Railway and also Deputy Chairman of the SER. Although Earl De La Warr had made such a strong request to join the CS&BR board, the company minute book shows that he perhaps surprisingly attended very few board meetings.

While all this was happening, the SER had finally ended many feuding years with their rivals the London Chatham & Dover Railway (LC&DR) by entering into an agreement whereby both companies would remain separate but would work together under the heading of the South Eastern & Chatham Railway Management Committee (SE&CR). This new arrangement took place from January 1st 1899 with Bonsor of the SER as Chairman and Aretas Akers-Douglas of the LC&DR as Deputy Chairman.

With construction of the CS&BR well under way, the most difficult and time consuming feature was of course the 17 arch viaduct spanning the valley and marshes for a length of 417 yards. It caused the contractors a great deal of trouble on several occasions owing to the subsidence of the embankments at either end. It was estimated that over nine million bricks were used in this very imposing structure. The turnings were of blue Staffordshire, and the rest was red brick.

The north abutment was started in December 1898, and the last arch was turned on September 21st 1900. Originally it was intended to construct the piers on piles driven into the earth, and a start was made, but the piles gave way. It was then decided to substitute huge concrete blocks, forming a stable foundation. The largest block near the Combe Haven stream was 32 ft. deep, and 52 ft. long by 30 ft. wide. The geological formation of the marsh at that time consisted of peat, soft bluish clay, and sandy greenish clay resting on a bed of shingle, beneath which lay a hard blue clay.

Below ground level, the piers were built to a depth of 40 ft. and above to the level of the railway the viaduct rose to a height of 67 ft., and the parapet was 4½ ft. The full height was 71½ ft., or, including that below the surface 111½ ft. When the viaduct was completed, the first actual engine to cross over it was the contractors Manning Wardle 0-6-0 saddle tank "Sidley", which was driven by Mr. Ben Brewington who was ably assisted by his 'stoker' Mr. W. Simmons.

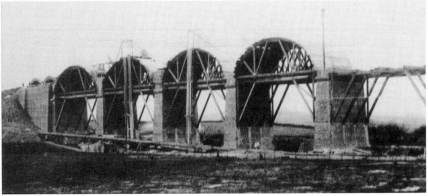

The viaduct while under construction.   Bexhill Museum

The completed viaduct, just before the line opened in 1902.   Bexhill-on-Sea Observer

There were two deep cuttings on the route. The first one was at Crowhurst on what was referred to as the south side of the big bank. 280,000 cubic yards of earth was removed from this cutting to form embankments in the vicinity although nothing was taken across the marsh from this part. The other deep cutting was at Sidley where 300,000 cubic yards of earth was excavated from the site where the station and station yard were built. The earth was taken from here to Bexhill to form the banks and foundations for the new line and terminus. Pipes were also laid along the route from the Combe Haven stream to the terminus at Bexhill where the locomotives could take water after it had been pumped from the stream.

Hunslet Engine Co. 0-6-0 saddle tank "Hastings" with the contractors workmen in the cutting at Sidley in 1902.
Bexhill-on-Sea Observer

Another view showing the cutting at Sidley.
Bexhill Museum

Manning Wardle 0-6-0 saddle tank "St. Leonards" on a temporary bridge structure.
Bexhill Museum

There were sixteen bridges on the route which included three over public roads plus iron footbridges at Crowhurst and Sidley stations and one near Worsham Manor.

The signalling arrangements were provided by Messrs. Evans, O'Donnell and Co., who were well know signal engineers of Westminster and Chippenham.

The three station buildings were rather grand for such a short line and in particular the terminus at Bexhill. The joint architects were C.S. Barry and C.E. Mercer and although we will look at the stations in more detail in the *Description of the Route* (pages 18 to 25) it is worth mentioning that Crowhurst Station was built in yellow and red brick with long and spacious platforms while the building at Sidley composed of red brick, slate roof, with Bath stone dressing. The terminus at Bexhill was a very imposing structure faced in red brick, with some very effective decorative work on the front of the main block, surmounted with an artistic clock tower under a small dome. Refreshment rooms in the building were let to Messrs. Spiers & Pond Ltd.

Bexhill Station soon after it was built. It later became Bexhill West in 1929. Authors Collection

A similar view of Sidley Station which was at road level with steps down to the platforms.
G. Dinnage Collection

Crowhurst Station at around the same time as the above views. Lens of Sutton

In 1900 it was also decided to build an approach road to Crowhurst Station from the village at a cost of £4,000 which was paid for by the SE&CR who also put up £4,184 for a hotel to be built near the station.

The line received the official inspection by Major J.W. Pringle on behalf of the Board of Trade on Friday April 25th 1902. The *Bexhill-on-Sea Observer* reported the event in their Saturday April 26th 1902 issue as follows:-

Yesterday (Friday) the official inspection by the Board of Trade took place, the Government Department responsible for the due examination and sanction of the line before its use by the public being represented by Major Pringle. Accompanied by several officials of the South Eastern Railway Company, he journeyed from London yesterday morning in a special train, arriving at Crowhurst about eleven o'clock, and returned from Bexhill last evening about six.

The special, consisting of a saloon, a first-class coach, and guard's compartment, was drawn by an eighty-five ton locomotive, being accompanied on the other set of rails by a similar engine. In addition to the Inspector, the company included Mr. Thompson, superintendent of the line; Mr. Butt, assistant engineer; Mr. Lennard, the telegraph superintendent. and his assistant, Mr. Packham; Mr. Barry, the engineer of the new railway; Mr. Price, the contractor; Mr. Bruce, resident engineer; and Mr. English, superintendent engineer of the works.

Commencing at Crowhurst, Major Pringle made a thorough inspection of the track, the Stations, the bridges and the magnificent viaduct spanning the Crowhurst Valley, besides the various other works connected with the new railway. On arrival at the Bexhill terminus the Inspector and railway officials drove to the Hotel Metropole for lunch, while Mr. English entertained some eight members of the party at the Pelham Hotel, Sidley. After a brief interregnum, the inspection of the Bexhill end of the line was proceeded with, Major Pringle concluding his observations and surveys about six o'clock, when the special train returned to London.

Major Pringle reported to the Board of Trade on April 28th 1902 and advised them to authorise the opening of the branch for passenger traffic, and while making very minor suggestions, approved of all particulars of construction and seemed most impressed with the viaduct.

The first appointed stationmaster at Bexhill was Mr. Cloake who was transferred from Grove Park while Mr.Trigg from Kemsing was the first stationmaster at Sidley and Mr. Nash from Dunton Green was the first stationmaster at Crowhurst.

The *Bexhill-on-Sea Observer* of Saturday May 17th 1902 proudly announced that the ceremonial opening of the new Bexhill Railway would be on Saturday week May 31st 1902 and that the line would be open to the public on the following day Sunday June 1st. The report also mentioned that this new excellent train service would take 1 hour 40 minutes to London and 1 hour 38 minutes from London.

The grand ceremonial opening was reported in the Saturday June 7th 1902 editions of both the local newspapers, the *Bexhill-on-Sea Observer* and the *Bexhill Chronicle* who made a strong point about how Bexhill had increased its importance in the past month with three major events, the first being the fact that the Urban Council had been raised in status to a Borough Council, the second being the unique automobile trials which had received world-wide attention and was to later give Bexhill the name of "The home of British Motor Racing". The third event was the opening of the new railway line. The report went on to say Bexhillians of the future will look back upon the Spring of 1902 with pride, and remark, "We gained these things in a few weeks; point us out any other instance like it".

The *Bexhill Chronicle* went on to report the opening as follows:-

THE OPENING DAY

On the opening day, last Saturday, the weather could hardly have been more favourable. Glorious sunshine prevailed all day, and at Bexhill it was beautifully summer-like. At the terminus things were early astir. Along either side of the road leading to the station were tall white flag poles with streamers and bannerettes fluttering from them, while the station itself was gay with bunting, flags, and patriotic mottoes and devices. A London firm had been engaged to decorate all three stations and their approaches, and they had done their work so well that everything seemed smothered in the national colours. In the large booking hall a table had been laid out, where the station employees were afterwards to have lunch at the same time as the larger function at the Hotel Metropole. Towards noon the officials and porters were bustling about preparing for the special train which was to leave at noon to join the Directors and guests coming from London Bridge, at Crowhurst Junction. It was no small affair which was prepared for this party, and yet before twelve o'clock every compartment of the train was occupied. The Urban Council was fully represented - all Bexhill, in fact, seemed to be there. Photographers were busy up and down the platforms, and porters were banging doors as though they had long ago got used to the hurry of the terminus, and crowds were at the station entrance and approaches - watching the scene. Exactly as the clocks were striking the hour, this first train glided out of Bexhill into Sidley Station, decorated in the same lavish way, and then over the viaduct on to Crowhurst, were it arrived at 12.10.

At Crowhurst the same curiosity prevailed, and people crowded on the footbridge overlooking the platform. The wait here was not long, for exactly at 12.30, just the time fixed, the special saloon train, which had left Charing Cross at 11.10 a.m. and London Bridge at 11.15, drew up at the Junction. Every seat in this had long ago been spoken for. Earl De La Warr and the Directors were there with all the important guests of the day, one or two Bexhillians including Mr. J.M. Glover, and several members of the London Press. The train was in charge of Mr. George Goodyer, traffic inspector, and the journey from London through the beautiful intervening country had been made without hitch. The directorate, forsooth, is generally sufficient guarantee of safety and punctuality in such excursions.

At Crowhurst a stop was made for the carriages which had brought up the other guests, to be affixed to the saloons, and then the rest of the journey was made at slow enough rate to give the guests an idea of the character of the construction of the new line.

THE ARRIVAL

Hundreds were at the terminus to watch the arrival of the train, and there was much enthusiasm as it glided into the gaily decked Station. Although the officials had kept the platforms clear and the best order prevailed, snap-shooters were dodging about all over the place, and there was too much of the obliquitous about them for their movements to be avoided. The Directors afterwards formed a group in the centre of the platform, and it became plain that a short speech of inauguration, so to speak, would have to be made.

Earl De La Warr, amid clapping, then stepped into an open space formed in the centre, and announced the Hon. A.E. Gathorne-Hardy would say a few words.

The Hon. A.E. Gathorne-Hardy said it gave him much pleasure to come to Bexhill and announce the opening of the new railway. There had been some difficulties to overcome before the present success was attained, and the line had cost a great deal of money. He was one of those who believed in the future of Bexhill (cheers), and in the future of this railway (renewed cheers). He hoped they would have a good return for the opening of the new line, and that a new era had begun for the town, which he hoped would grow into one of the greatest health resorts on the South Coast (cheers).

The Hon. A.E. Gathorne-Hardy (back to camera) declaring the new line open.

Bexhill-on-Sea Observer

The London visitors then inspected the station premises and all agreed that they were a credit to the Company and a great acquisition to Bexhill. As mentioned in the *Bexhill Chronicle* report, large tables were laid for a luncheon in the booking hall for the station staff and other railway employees while the main luncheon was held at the Hotel Metropole under the able management of Mr. Charles Colomb. Several carriages were provided to convey the guests to the hotel, although the majority preferred to walk.

The president of the gathering was the Chairman of the CS&BR the Hon. A.E. Gathorne-Hardy who was introduced to Mr. Colomb by Earl De La Warr. Apart from all the other directors and officials of the CS&BR (with the exception of Mr. Pelham Rawston Papillon who was doing his duty in South Africa) the guest list included some of the most influential railways officials and politicians of the day with all the main participants of the SE&CR ranging from Mr. H. Cosmo O. Bonsor (Chairman), the Right Hon. Aretas Akers-Douglas M.P. (Deputy Chairman) who was also the Conservative Home Secretary from 1902 to 1905, other SE&CR directors like Lord Burton, Lord Hothfield, Sir Alfred M. Watkin, Sir Myles Fenton, the Right Hon. Sir William Hart-Dyke M.P. and Mr. William Mewburn plus many other leading officials including Mr. Vincent Hill (General Manager), Mr. Harry S. Wainwright (Locomotive Superintendent) and Mr. Charles Sheath (Secretary to the SE&CR and the CS&BR). From the LB&SCR came director the Right Hon. Sir A. Otway, Sir Charles Morgan (Engineer), and Sir William Forbes (General Manager) while from the London & North West Railway came their Solicitor Mr. C.H. Mason.

The ceremonial first train at the new Bexhill terminus.   Bexhill Chronicle

Carriages were laid on at the new station to take the special guests to the Hotel Metropole for the main luncheon. Some were happy to walk.   Bexhill Chronicle

One of the other railway personalities invited was Mr. Holman F. Stephens who had been the engineer responsible for the recently constructed Rother Valley Railway which was a light railway that ran from Robertsbridge (three stops north of Crowhurst on the main Hastings - Tonbridge line) to Tenterden in Kent. A similar light railway had also been planned in 1899 to run from Robertsbridge to Pevensey although, it was never built. The engineer named for this line was surprisingly not Stephens (who went on to build and manage many other light railways) but one of the CS&BR engineers Arthur John Barry.

Also present at the luncheon was Mr. J. Henniker Heaton M.P. for Canterbury and a long time resident of Bexhill, the Mayor of Hastings Alderman Langham and the Mayor of Eastbourne Alderman N. Strange along with many members of the Hastings, Eastbourne and Bexhill Councils. At this time, the provisional Mayor for the new Bexhill Borough Council was none other than Earl De La Warr.

The luncheon commenced at 1.45 p.m. after grace had been given by the Rector of Crowhurst the Rev. J.P. Bacon-Phillips. The Hon. A. Gathorne-Hardy briefly gave the loyal toasts to "The King", "Queen Alexandra, the Prince and Princess of Wales, and other members of the Royal Family". Mr. J. Henniker Heaton M.P. proposed "The Crowhurst, Sidley and Bexhill Railway" and was responded to by the Hon. A.E. Gathorne-Hardy. Earl De La Warr proposed "The South Eastern and Chatham Railway Management Committee" and was responded to by Mr. H.C.O. Bonsor. The Right Hon. Sir W. Hart-Dyke M.P. proposed "The Mayor and Corporation of Bexhill" and was responded to by the Deputy Mayor of Bexhill Mr. Daniel Mayer J.P. and also Mr. W.J. Smith J.P. Mr. Vincent Hill proposed "The Engineers and Contractors" and was responded to by Mr. A.J. Barry and Mr. J. Price. The Hon. A. E. Gathorne-Hardy proposed "The Visitors" and was responded to by the Mayor of Eastbourne Alderman N. Strange and Mr. W. Forbes of the LB&SCR, and finally Sir Anchitel Piers Ashburnham-Clement proposed "The Chairman" and was responded to by the Hon. A.E. Gathorne-Hardy.

Almost immediately after the dinner, everyone made their way back to the new station where at 4.30 p.m. the special saloon train started to steam out just as Sir W. Hart-Dyke and another gentleman arrived on the platform. The train quickly stopped to pick them up and then as crowds of people waited at the entrances and approaches of the station, to see the departure, the train once again steamed out to loud cheers, hand shakes and hats lifted. With just one stop at Tunbridge Wells, the memorable excursion reached London Bridge at about 6 p.m. Several of the next day editions of the London newspapers gave accounts of the new railway at Bexhill.

A group of the special guests gather on the platform at Bexhill (left) while Mr. Cloake the stationmaster and other staff watch a SE&CR inspector read despatches (right). Bexhill-on-Sea Observer

The following day, Sunday June 1st 1902, the line was opened to the public and the new railway seems to have soon settled down to the general day to day running. In the same year that the line opened, an agreement was signed with the Anglo-American Oil Company for use by that company of tanks and sidings at Bexhill.

The following article appeared in the July 1902 edition of the *Railway Magazine* describing with great enthusiasm the service offered by the new line:-

Mr. Vincent Hill, the General Manager of the South-Eastern and Chatham Railway, has provided an excellent train service over the new line, and it remains for the residents of Bexhill and the numerous visitors to that charming resort to show their appreciation of the boon that has been conferred upon them by extensively patronising the new railway. This they should readily do, as the distance from London to Bexhill by the South-Eastern and Chatham route is only 62 miles compared with 71 miles by the London, Brighton and South Coast Railway. The train service is most liberal, there being thirteen down and thirteen up trains on week days; of these, one up and one down are through express trains to Charing Cross and Cannon Street, stopping only at Tunbridge Wells, Sidley, and Bexhill, the total time on the journey from Cannon Street occupying but 1 hour 39 minutes. In addition to the through expresses, there are four up and three down trains having through carriages; of these, one down and two up are to Charing Cross, the other two, both up and down, are to Victoria, the journey to which station is performed in 1 hour 48 minutes.

The Sunday services is also most liberal, and includes an express with through carriages from Victoria in 1 hour 46 minutes, and there is a return express in the evening.

In 1905, the Hon. A.E. Gathorne-Hardy was appointed a Railway Commissioner and resigned his seat on the CS&BR board. The new chairman was Col. John James Mellor although, as expected, the CS&BR soon ceased to exist and was absorbed by the SE&CR as from January 1st 1907.

The seventeen arch viaduct in 1918.   J.E. Cope Collection

The new station at Bexhill soon after the line had opened.   G. Dinnage Collection

Despite the optimistic beginnings with the quicker route to London and the rather grand stations on the new line, many passengers still seemed to favour the LB&SCR station and the original route. Matters were not helped during the first World War when a directive from the Railway Executive Committee requested that the branch (like many other branch lines) be closed as an economy measure and passenger services were withdrawn from January 1st 1917. Although goods trains started to operate again from November 5th 1917, full passenger services were not reinstated to Bexhill until March 1st 1919 while Sidley surprisingly remained closed to passengers until June 14th 1920. To try and tempt passengers back, through trains to London were quickly restored.

After the 1923 grouping, the SE&CR became part of the newly formed Southern Railway who by inheriting the former LB&SCR and SE&CR stations suddenly had two stations at Bexhill. Just to confuse matters the SE&CR station had been opened as Bexhill-on-Sea even though the LB&SCR station was actually nearer to the sea. To overcome this matter the former LB&SCR station was named Bexhill Central from July 9th 1923 while the former SE&CR station became simply Bexhill until it received its final name of Bexhill West in November 1929.

Although some through trains to London had been re-introduced, the Southern Railway arranged that most main line trains calling at Crowhurst would include three corridor carriages for Bexhill West although this failed to attract passengers away from the former LB&SCR route where, even though it took longer they could still reach London without changing.

In 1930, planning consultants Messrs. Adams, Thompson and Fry were asked by the Town Council to produce a report on the general development of Bexhill. What they proposed was to connect the two railway lines by building a loop from the head of the West Station goods yard crossing over Terminus Road and joining the Central Station line near Sackville Arch. The consultants also suggested a new Central Station on the goods yard at Buckhurst Place with a station entrance fronting on to the Town Hall Square. Although nothing came of this plan, it is interesting to note that while the CS&BR was under construction, it was briefly linked with the LB&SCR when the latter company agreed for the CS&BR contractors Price & Reeves to connect with their sidings at Bexhill by laying a temporary track so that chalk could be conveyed from Glynde to the new line. Once the task had been completed, the temporary track was removed.

Ganger Fred Hutchinson at work on the line.
J.E. Cope Collection

Gangers Tom Pullen (left), Tom Woolard (centre) and Mr. Izzard (right).
J.E. Cope Collection

In 1935 the former LB&SCR coastal line was electrified and from then on the Southern Railway seemed to have considered it as their main London line from Bexhill while the former CS&BR line from Bexhill West was seen more as a branch.

In 1937 the Southern Railway proposed a scheme for electrification of the main Hastings line and this also included the Bexhill West branch. Special stock was to be provided to fit the main line's restricted loading gauge. Unlike the former LB&SCR line, this scheme came to nothing, but if it had, it might well have given the branch a long term future.

From the late 1930's, pull-and-push trains started working the line and replacing some of the through carriages and, by the mid 1940's they took over completely when the through carriages were withdrawn.

After nationalisation in 1948, the Southern Railway passed into the hands of the British Railways Southern Region.

In 1949 the line, which was now very much referred to as a branch, took on for a brief period the full importance of a main line when Bopeep tunnel on the main line had to be closed for very extensive repairs. The work lasted from November 27th 1949 until June 4th 1950 which necessitated all main line trains from London to Hastings to terminate at Bexhill West.

'Schools' V Class 4-4-0 No. 30905 *Tonbridge* crossing the viaduct with the main line Charing Cross to Bexhill West train. April 22nd 1950.   S.C. Nash

Once the tunnel was repaired and normal service was resumed, the pull-and-push trains again were restored to a normal timetable and this arrangement lasted until June 1958 when they were replaced by two-car diesel-electric units which connected with the London to Hastings diesel-electric trains at Crowhurst. Even then steam briefly returned to the branch in March 1959 due to a shortage of diesel stock. Also, during this time, an unadvertised school train ran between Etchingham and Bexhill West.

The Sunday winter service was withdrawn from January 3rd to April 10th 1960 and was never reinstated. From this time onwards fears grew for the future of the line and when the Beeching Report was published on March 27th 1963, the Bexhill West branch was one of the lines recommended for closure. Originally the line should have closed on September 9th 1963 when the goods service was withdrawn but after much discussion, the line finally closed to all traffic on and from June 15th 1964.

Description of the Route

The line to Bexhill started from a junction on the main London - Hastings line at Crowhurst where the station was built and opened to the public on June 1st 1902, the same time as the new line. Situated about two miles south of Battle and four miles north of West St. Leonards, the layout at Crowhurst consisted of four through tracks, two of which were for stopping trains while the centre two were for up and down through express trains. The two 600 ft long and 25 ft wide platforms also accommodated bays for the Bexhill line which were approached from the south of the station. Trains from Bexhill arrived at the up bay to await the arrival of an up main line train and then would be shunted across to the down bay to be ready for the next down main line train.

The main station building on the up side was constructed in yellow and red brick and consisted of a booking hall, ticket office, comfortable ladies' waiting room and toilet, stationmaster's office, porters' room and a gents' toilet. A large platform canopy was also provided. The platforms were connected by a lattice girder footbridge. The station building on the down side was similar in appearance to the one on the up side and was about the same length but was not so deep. It also had a large canopy and consisted of a general waiting room, a ladies' waiting room and toilet and a gents' toilet.

Signal boxes were provided at both ends of the station. The No. 1 box was situated on the down side approach to the station from the north while No. 2 box was also on the down side but to the south of the station where the line to Bexhill branched away.

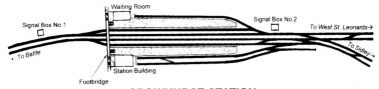

CROWHURST STATION

The approach from the road to Crowhurst Station on May 11th 1957.   Denis Cullum

18

Looking south from the footbridge at Crowhurst Station. May 11th 1957.   Denis Cullum

Passengers from Bexhill and Sidley wait at Crowhurst for their connection to London having just arrived in the diesel electric unit which is in the up bay. May 18th 1964.   G.R. Croughton

H class 0-4-4T No. 31162 draws across to the down bay platform at Crowhurst to form the 3.47 p.m. train to Bexhill West. April 12th 1958.   D.W. Winkworth

H class 0-4-4T No. 31295 approaching Crowhurst with the 12.20 p.m. train from Bexhill West. May 11th 1957.

From Crowhurst the line to Bexhill descended at 1 in 90 while crossing over a small country lane by bridge before entering into a cutting and passing under a small road bridge near Sampson's Farm and then under another small road bridge near the entrance to Adams Farm. Nearby, an 18" gauge tramway ran for about 500 yards to one of the Hastings Corporation waterworks.

The line to Bexhill continued the descent at 1 in 100 before reaching the 17 arch viaduct on the level. As we have already read, the viaduct which crossed the valley, marshes and the Combe Haven stream was the major engineering feat of the line and passengers crossing over it were offered wonderful views of the countryside which stretched for miles.

From the viaduct the line continued on the level before starting to climb up the far side of the valley towards Sidley at 1 in 170. At this point the line passed under a small footbridge known locally as the 'iron bridge' which was used for a footpath leading to the nearby Worsham Manor and Farm.

After passing through Combe Wood the line started to descend once again at 1 in 100 and crossed over yet another small lane by bridge before passing Glovers Farm and under the same lane by bridge.

Looking across to the viaduct from the main Hastings line. May 11th 1957.

H class 0-4-4T No. 31269 propels pull-and-push unit No. 651 over the viaduct on the way to Bexhill. March 2nd 1955.   Denis Cullum

The same train having just left the viaduct. March 2nd 1955.   Denis Cullum

Pull-and-push unit No. 661 with H class 0-4-4T No. 31162 south of the viaduct which can be seen on the left of the photograph. March 2nd 1955.   Denis Cullum

The line continued in a cutting and passed under a bridge at Sidley Road before arriving at Sidley Station which was also in a cutting and was about 3 miles 25 chains from Crowhurst on a falling gradient of 1 in 260. When opened, the main station building, which was red brick and Bath stone dressing with a slate roof, consisted of a booking office, general waiting room, ladies' waiting room and toilet, ticket and parcels office, gents' toilet and stationmaster's office. It was actually situated at road level next to the bridge and opposite the Pelham Hotel. Passengers would buy their tickets and leave the station building at the back of the booking office and then down a few steps to a lattice girder footbridge similar to the one at Crowhurst with a flight of steps leading to each platform.

Both platforms were 490 ft long and were originally provided with waiting rooms with fireplaces, the buildings were of wood on brick foundations. In 1938 the Southern Railway decided to let the road level station building and transfer the booking office to the waiting room on the up platform. Near the Bexhill end of the down platform was the signal box which contained 20 levers while on the opposite side trailing off the up line was the goods yard and sidings. A large shed was provided which proved a success in the early years of the line but was sold out of use by the Southern Railway in 1929.

[Diagram: SIDLEY STATION — showing ←To Crowhurst, Original Station Building, Waiting Room, Signal Box, Waiting Room & Booking Office, Footbridge, Goods Shed, To Bexhill→]

SIDLEY STATION

The original station building at Sidley while in use as a garage. June 14th 1964.   S.C. Nash

Looking north towards Crowhurst from the down platform at Sidley Station.   G. Dinnage Collection

Sidley Station, looking south from the road bridge. March 2nd 1955.   Denis Cullum

The line continued on a falling gradient of 1 in 100 but as a contrast from the rural scenery between Crowhurst and Sidley, the route from Sidley to Bexhill continued in suburban surroundings and passed under a bridge at Woodsgate Park and over a subway before crossing on a level gradient over the Down Road bridge and falling again at 1 in 93 before reaching the terminus at Bexhill West on the level. The Down Road bridge not only crossed over Down Road but also Little Common Road, the central support falling between the two roads at the junction.

The bridge which crossed over Down Road and Little Common Road.   Bexhill-on-Sea Observer

The station building at Bexhill West which was approached from Terminus Road was the largest and most imposing of the three fine station buildings on the line and contained a very impressive clock tower. The front of the building with its red faced brick, Bath stone dressing and Welsh slate roof gave a rather grand appearance especially over the entrance which featured a block-moulded pediment which was carved in situ. The main building consisted of a large and lofty booking hall, ticket and parcels offices, a general waiting room which also included a ladies' waiting room and toilet plus the stationmaster's and inspectors' offices. A smaller block which was placed at right angles to the main building contained the refreshment room, gents' toilet, porters' and lamp rooms.

There were two island platforms, 700 ft in length and 30 ft wide of which the eastern one (platform 1 and 2) was covered with a glass roof, resting on an iron structure for a distance of 400 ft. The area covered by the glass roof was paved while the exposed part of platform was gravelled. The 40 ft by 90 ft covered space which lay between the station buildings was covered in a similar manner to the eastern island platform. Next to platform 1 was a loop siding while between platforms 2 and 3 were three tracks, the centre one being an engine release track.

The approach to Bexhill West Station from Terminus Road. July 28th 1953.   R.C. Riley

The western island platform which made up platform 3 and what would have been platform 4 was not covered and to make things worse, platform 4 never actually received a track. Platform 3 was soon to be rarely used by passengers and was quickly covered by grass. Although the station buildings were lit by electricity, the platforms were surprisingly lit by gas and remained so until the line closed.

Signal box No. 1 covered the extensive station yard and had 123 levers, 80 of which were working. To the east of the station was a large goods shed which housed two 30 cwt cranes. A larger 4 ton 2 cwt crane was provided in the yard which also had extensive coal and cattle pens. On the west side of the station were four carriage sidings and a two track 119 ft by 32 ft engine shed with a coal stage and a 54 ft 9 in turntable. The engine shed was originally a sub shed of Hastings until 1929 when it came under the control of St. Leonards. In 1938 it was taken out of use and was sold to Hall & Co. who used it from then on as a warehouse.

Signal box No. 2 was surprisingly positioned between the buffer stop ends of platforms 2 and 3 and had 22 levers of which 12 were working.

H class 0-4-4T No. 31162 with the branch train at Bexhill West Station. Signal box No. 2 can be seen at the end of the middle track behind the buffers. April 12th 1958.   D.W. Winkworth

The entrance gate to platforms 1 and 2.   G. Dinnage Collection

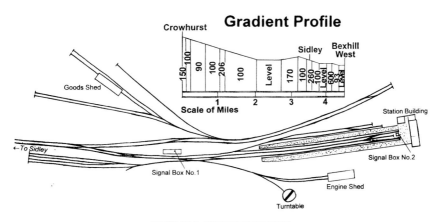

Gradient Profile

Crowhurst
Sidley
Bexhill West

Goods Shed

←To Sidley

Signal Box No.1

Turntable

Station Building

Signal Box No.2

Engine Shed

Scale of Miles

BEXHILL WEST STATION

Looking south towards the station platforms at Bexhill West. The engine shed is on the right of the photograph.   P. Gavin/G. Dinnage Collection

H class 0-4-4T No. 31161 shunting empty stock by signal box No. 1. March 26th 1959. S.C. Nash

25

Motive Power and Rolling Stock

With several through express trains running between Bexhill and London when the new line opened, the motive power appears to have been mainly worked by SE&CR 4-4-0 tender engines designed by former SER Locomotive Superintendent James Stirling and Harry S. Wainwright who succeeded Stirling when the SE&CR was formed.

After the decline of the through London service in the late 1930's, two carriage pull-and-push trains worked by former LB&SCR D3 class 0-4-4T's (designed by R.J. Billinton the LB&SCR Locomotive Superintendent from 1890 to 1905) took over the branch duties, and were provided from the shed at St. Leonards. The D3's were later to give way to the ever faithful Wainwright H class 0-4-4T's until they were replaced in June 1958 by two-car diesel-electric trains. At about this time, one goods train visited the branch daily, usually pulled by a Bulleid Q1 class 0-6-0 provided from Tonbridge but sometimes from St. Leonards. This duty was later handled by a 03 class 0-6-0 diesel.

As mentioned in the history of the line, when the Bopeep tunnel on the main line was closed from November 1949 until June 1950 for extensive repairs, all the main line trains from London to Hastings were temporarily diverted to Bexhill West, which meant that a whole variety of main line locomotives could be seen on the branch.

D3 class 0-4-4T No. 32388 at Bexhill West Station. July 15th 1950.   R.C. Riley

H class 0-4-4T No. 31295 also seen at Bexhill West Station. July 27th 1955.   R.M. Casserley

Schools' V Class 4-4-0 No. 30933 *King's Canterbury* heading towards Sidley after crossing the viaduct with the main line Cannon Street to Bexhill West train. April 22nd 1950.   S.C. Nash

Q1 Class 0-6-0 No. 33028 passing through Sidley Station with empty stock for Bexhill West. April 22nd 1957.   D.W. Winkworth

Diesel electric unit No. 1121 at Bexhill West Station. November 19th 1958.   Alan A. Jackson

Timetables and Tickets

JUNE 1902

DOWN				Week Days									T		
	a.m.	a.m.	a.m.	a.m.	a.m.	p.m.	p.m.	p.m.	p.m.	p.m.	p.m.	p.m.	p.m.	p.m.	p.m.
Crowhurst	7.25	8.20	8.50	10.50	11.23	12.10	1. 8	2.54	4.15	5.36	6.55	7.25	.....	8.40	9.20
Sidley	7.31	8.26	8.56	10.56	11.29	12.16	1.14	3. 0	4.21	5.42	.....	7.31	7.24	8.46	9.26
Bexhill	7.35	8.30	9. 0	11. 0	11.33	12.20	1.18	3. 4	4.25	5.46	7. 3	7.37	7.27	8.50	9.30

DOWN				Sundays				
	a.m.	a.m.	a.m.	p.m.	p.m.	p.m.	p.m.	p.m.
Crowhurst	9.42	10.45	11.27	12.08	5.10	5.55	8.25	9.46
Sidley	9.48	10.51	11.33	12.13	5.15	6. 0	8.30	9.51
Bexhill	9.52	10.55	11.37	11.17	5.19	6. 4	8.34	9.55

UP	A	B		T	Week Days										
	a.m.	a.m.	a.m.	a.m.	a.m.	a.m.	p.m.	p.m.	p.m.	p.m.	p.m.	p.m.	p.m.	p.m.	p.m.
Bexhill	6.58	7. 5	8. 0	8.50	10.15	11.51	12.42	2.19	3.54	4.52	6. 0	7.18	7. 3	9. 7	
Sidley	7. 1	7. 8	8. 3	8.53	10.18	11.54	12.45	2.22	3.57	4.55	6. 3	7.21	8. 1	9.10	
Crowhurst	7. 9	7.16	8.11	......	10.26	12.02	12.53	2.30	4. 5	5. 3	6.11	7.29	8. 9	9.17	

UP			Sundays				Week Days	
	a.m.	a.m.	p.m.	p.m.	p.m.	p.m.		
Bexhill	6.50	10.24	4.52	5.40	8. 7	9. 5	T Through Trains.	A Mondays Only.
Sidley	6.53	10.27	4.55	5.43	8.10	9. 8	B Not Mondays.	
Crowhurst	7. 1	10.35	5. 3	5.51	8.18	9.16		

JULY 1922

DOWN						Week Days					S			N			S Saturdays Only
	a.m.	a.m.	a.m.	a.m.	a.m.	a.m.	p.m.	p.m.	p.m.	p.m.	p.m.	p.m.	p.m.	p.m.	p.m.	p.m.	N Not after 8th instance
Crowhurst	7.15	8.30	8.30	10.15	11. 2	11.55	12.30	2. 0	2.47	2.52	3.59	4. 9	5.15	5.52			
Sidley	7.21	8.36	8.36	10.21	11. 8	12. 1	12.36	2. 6	2.53	2.58	3. 6	4. 5	4.15	5.21	5.58		
Bexhill	7.25	8.40	8.40	10.25	11.12	12. 5	12.40	2.10	2.57	3. 2	3.10	4. 9	4.19	5.25	6. 2		

DOWN	S	Week Days *Continued*			W					Sundays							
	p.m.	p.m.	p.m.	p.m.	p.m.	p.m.	p.m.	p.m.		a.m.	a.m.	a.m.	a.m.	p.m.	p.m.	p.m.	p.m. p.m. p.m.
Crowhurst	6.32	6.38	......	7.25	7.50	8.25	9. 5	11. 4		7.25	9.40	10.22	11. 0	11.42	12.47	5.20	6.20 7. 5 10. 5
Sidley	6.38	6.44	6.50	7.31	7.56	8.31	9.11	11.20		7.31	9.46	10.28	11. 6	11.49	12.53	5.26	6.26 7.11 10.11
Bexhill	6.42	6.48	6.54	7.35	8. 0	8.35	9.15	11.26		7.35	9.50	10.32	11.10	11.53	12.57	5.30	6.30 7.15 10.15

UP						Week Days				S	E	S	S	E		E Except Saturdays
	a.m.	a.m.	a.m.	a.m.	a.m.	a.m.	p.m.	p.m.	p.m.	p.m.	p.m.	p.m.	p.m.	p.m.		W Wednesdays & Saturdays
Bexhill	6.55	7.35	8.10	9. 5	9.45	10.30	11. 0	11.40	12.12	1.30	1.45	2.30	3.25	3.35	4.55	
Sidley	6.57	7.37	8.12	9. 7	9.47	10.32	11. 2	11.42	12.14	1.32	1.47	2.32	3.27	3.37	4.57	
Crowhurst	7. 5	7.45	8.20	.....	9.55	10.40	11.10	11.50	12.22	1.40	1.55	2.40	3.35	3.45	5. 5	

UP		Week Days *Continued*				Sundays								
	p.m.	p.m.	p.m.	p.m.	p.m.	a.m.	a.m.	a.m.	a.m.	p.m.	p.m.	p.m.	p.m.	p.m. p.m.
Bexhill	5.32	6.15	7. 5	8. 5	8.45	7. 0	9. 5	10. 0	10.40	11.20	12.10	5. 0	6. 0	6.35 8. 0
Sidley	5.34	6.17	7. 7	8. 7	8.47	7. 2	9. 7	10. 2	10.42	11.22	12.12	5. 2	6. 2	6.37 8. 2
Crowhurst	5.42	6.25	7.15	8.15	8.55	7.10	9.15	10.10	10.50	11.30	12.20	5.10	6.10	6.45 8.10

Tickets from the G.R. Croughton Collection.

Closure

With any thoughts finally gone of the Bexhill West line ever being anything more than a branch, it must have seemed that this short line with three grand stations plus the viaduct had become a rather expensive white elephant. With Doctor Beeching drawing up plans in the early 1960's to close all uneconomic railways, fears that the line could be considered proved to be right. The first public announcement of the intention of closure came in the *Beeching Report on the reshaping of British Railways* on March 27th 1963. The original closure date was given as September 9th 1963 when the goods service was in fact withdrawn and a better service from St. Leonards was promised plus a bus service to connect Bexhill West and Sidley stations.

With over 200 season ticket holders making regular use of the line from Bexhill West and about 40 from Sidley it is not surprising that they formed the basis of the opposition to the closure and quickly formed the Hastings, Bexhill and District Season Ticket Holders Association. An inquiry was soon held by the Transport Users Consultative Committee for the South Eastern Area at Bexhill Town Hall, where a petition of 1,000 names was handed in. With a warning of hardship which would cost regular travellers at least five extra hours a week travel, there was a delay in closure but finally the date was given as June 14th 1964.

The June 20th 1964 edition of the *Hastings and St. Leonards Observer* mentioned the closure as follows:-

The Last Train From Bexhill West - and It Was Packed

The last train from Bexhill West to Crowhurst was packed when it left at 10.20 p.m. on Sunday, bringing to an end the regular hourly service, increased during business hours and on Sunday, which had been operating between the two stations for many years.

The Crowhurst Stationmaster. Mr. L.A. Pentecost, was among the passengers on the train. Regular passengers who used the line, axed by the Beeching Plan because there is an alternative route to London, also travelled on the last train.

Many commuters used the line to travel to London, but now they will have to go to Bexhill Central and change at Warrior-square, St. Leonards.

Many people are bringing their cars from Bexhill and leaving them at Crowhurst Station while they complete their journey to London and elsewhere.

There are car parking facilities for 34 cars at the station and there has been an average of 40 cars parked there at the beginning of this week.

Diesel electric units No's. 1007 and 1120 forming the 11.50 a.m. which is seen leaving Bexhill West for Crowhurst on July 14th 1964, the last day of public service.　　　S.C. Nash

Two passengers on the last train had actually made the first journey in 1902, they were Mr. William Knowles of 22 Salisbury Road, Bexhill and Mr. H.W. Hunt of 22 Grange Court Drive, Bexhill.

Leading Porter John Gray with Mr. Knowles and Mr. Hunt (who were both on the first train in 1902) at the barrier as it closed for the last time.

Guard John Heath waves his flag sending the last passenger train from Bexhill West Station on June 14th 1964. Bexhill-on-Sea Observer

The driver on this special final occasion was Len Larkin who had worked on the branch for many years. When the author made an appeal for local knowledge of the line, one of Mr. Larkin's daughters, Mrs. P. Hunnisett of Bexhill, kindly wrote the following interesting letter about her father which is reproduced below:-

I read with interest your notice in the Bexhill Observer asking for information about the Bexhill West railway.

My father, Len Larkin, had his moment of fame, after years of chugging up and down, when he was chosen to drive the last engine between Bexhill and Crowhurst and back again, with the Mayor, Corporation, and other Dignitaries aboard. There was great publicity, but my father wanted nothing of it and just came home. Of course, by this time, it was a diesel, and not an imposing steam engine.

He was based at Bopeep, Marina, Hastings, so he also drove to Charing Cross and Ashford. Although everyone thought our little line was boring, and had a rude name for it, as long as he was chuffing along in his beloved engine, he was still the schoolboy reliving his dream.

To his disappointment, he had four daughters. To us his engines were loud, dirty, and dangerous, but he was so proud of them. If we were travelling on his train, one by one we had to ride with him. We had to stand still because everything was red-hot (his boots had studs but still burnt through) the fire roared, the engine clanked and the poor fireman madly shovelled coal. How relieved we were to return to our seats. Imagine a boy feeling like that. It broke his heart when he transferred to diesels.

One day during the last war, a German fighter flew along the track and machined-gunned his train as it was crossing the viaduct. All he could think of was to drive at top speed, I don't think anyone was hurt.

There was a wonderful buffet at Bexhill West Station, a meeting place for everyone around. He liked to drop in there after his shift, for his little tot of whisky. Everyone knew Len Larkin.

The circus came to town one day and unloaded at the West Station. The elephants made such a mess but Dad swore that the allotment on the railway bank had never grown such wonderful produce.

There was a tremendous turntable by the station which would slowly reverse the engine. There was also a coal yard by the bridge which went over Little Common and Down roads joining the rail to Sidley.

Len Larkin prepares to drive the last train out of Bexhill West Station for the final trip. Bexhill-on-Sea Observer

The Present Scene

After the line closed in 1964 there were several attempts to have it reopened but all to no avail. The track was lifted in 1965 and that also included the bays and fast through tracks at Crowhurst. The bridge which crossed over Little Common and Down roads was demolished in 1967 and then in May 1969 with great publicity, the viaduct was dramatically blown up with a large crowd gathering on the Crowhurst marshes to witness the event.

Looking at the remains of the line at the time of writing, the fine station buildings at Crowhurst on the main line have been removed and facilities here are now rather basic. The original branch line bays at the south end of the station are still visible although very overgrown. Much of the former route of the branch is intact and can be walked in parts between Crowhurst and Sidley even though the viaduct has been removed. The road bridge at Sidley still remains while the former station building which adjoined the bridge and was later used as a petrol garage was demolished in early 1970 and replaced by a new petrol garage. The former goods shed at Sidley which the Southern Railway sold in 1929 is still standing but is not in very good condition.

The road bridge between Sidley and Bexhill at Woodsgate Park still remains while the fine station building at Bexhill West is still very evident and now serving as Gorringes Auction Galleries. To the east side of the building is the aptly named Dr. Beeching's pub and restaurant. The original engine shed is still standing although like the rest of the former station yard it now forms part of an industrial estate.

The viaduct being dramatically blown up In May 1969.   Bexhill Museum

The very overgrown up bay at Crowhurst Station. November 22nd 2000.   Author

The former goods shed at the site of Sidley Station. November 22nd 2000.   Author

The former Bexhill West Station now in use as Gorringes Auction Galleries. November 22nd 2000.   Author

Dr. Beeching's Pub & Restaurant. November 22nd 2000.   Author

Conclusion

The new line to Bexhill was opened with great celebrations in 1902 and if it had been the first and only line to the town, there is no doubt it would still be open. Unfortunately, the railway (in the shape of the LB&SCR) had already reached Bexhill with a more central station many years before, and even if it took longer to travel to the capital city by the original route, most of the passengers seemed reluctant to change. If (as was suggested) there had been a physical link between the two lines things may have been different.

It seems very strange that the SER (later SE&CR) were prepared to spend so much of their money in helping the CS&BR build this line although they probably saw it as a way of getting a stronger hold in Sussex and more importantly LB&SCR territory.

As with all closed railways, it would be interesting to look back at the opening day and the celebrations which took place and wonder what all those people would say today if they could only see what has happened to the line which they saw opened in 1902 with such enthusiasm.

Acknowledgements

I would like to thank the following people and organisations for their kind help in compiling information and supplying photographs for this publication: Mr. D. Cullum, Mr. S.C. Nash, Mr D.W. Winkworth Mr. R.M. Casserley, Mr. R.C. Riley, Mr. A.A. Jackson, Mr. G. Dinnage, Mr. J.E. Cope, Mr. G.R. Croughton, Mrs. P. Hunnisett, the librarians and staff at Bexhill Library, the staff at Bexhill Museum, the Bexhill-on-Sea Observer, the Public Records Office at Kew and of course the late Mr. J.L. Smith of Lens of Sutton.

My grateful thanks to Norman Branch for reading and checking my text and also to James Christian of Binfield Printers Ltd.

Bibliography

BRANCH LINES OF THE SOUTHERN RAILWAY Vol. 1 by George Reeve & Chris Hawkins (Wild Swan)
FORGOTTEN RAILWAYS: SOUTH-EAST ENGLAND by H.P. White (David & Charles)
THE RAILWAYS OF SOUTHERN ENGLAND: SECONDARY AND BRANCH LINES by Edwin Course (Batsford)
BEXHILL'S LOST ROUTE TO LONDON by Alan A. Jackson (Railways South East. The Album. 1994 Capital Transport Publishing)

Diesel electric units No's. 1007 and 1120 passing through Sidley Station forming the 11.5 a.m. from Crowhurst to Bexhill West on the last day of public service. July 14th 1964.   S.C. Nash